THE mizz BOOK OF
EMBARRASSING MOMENTS!

Text copyright © Panini UK Ltd 2009
Illustrations: Joanna Baldock.
Copyright © Panini UK Ltd 2009
Cover photography: Shareen Akhtar

With special thanks to:
Emily Conradi, Laura Jones, Lucy Saxton, Lisa Clark, Joanna Baldock,
Kate Miller, Gwennan Thomas, Darren Miles, Carol Bateup, Nick Clark

Published in Great Britain in 2009
by Panini Books

A catalogue record of this book is available from the
British Library.

ISBN: 978-1-84653-086-9

Printed and bound in England by Clays Ltd, St Ives plc

Panini Books a division of Panini UK Ltd.
Brockbourne House, 77 Mount Ephraim, Tunbridge Wells, Kent, TN4 8BS

Virgin pulp used during manufacture of the paper has been sourced
from sustainably managed forests certified by the Pan European Forest
Certification (PEFC) organisation.

Contents

Blush-o-meter

●○○○○ Gotta laugh
●●○○○ Oh dear
●●●○○ "It wasn't me"
●●●●○ Hide quick
●●●●● Argh!

Too saucy!

I went out to the cinema with my mates and then we decided to go for fast food. I ordered a super-size burger with extra ketchup and some ice cream. As I prepared to tuck in, I tore the sauce sachet open and it spurted out everywhere! Worst of all, big blobs of it landed in my ice cream so I couldn't eat it. Yuk!

Dee, London

Diary diss

My friend Abigail came to my place for a sleepover and, the next morning, she woke up earlier than I did. She found my diary, which I'd left lying around, and sneaked a peek at it. Unfortunately, though, it was a complete Bridget Jones moment, as she found a page where I'd written "I hate Abigail!" after a stupid fallout! I had to pretend that I'd used it in a game of make-believe with my little sis and that she'd written it!

Sophie, Basingtoke

Movie 'mare

My bezzie was going to the cinema with her bro and his mates, and I invited myself along, too, 'cause a couple of the lads were well lush! She and I spent ages making ourselves look glam and older so we would get in 'cause it was an 18-rated film. When we got to the desk to buy the ticket, the cashier took one look at me and said, "Nice try, little girl!' He then recommended I see really childish cartoon instead! The boys were not impressed!

Eloise, Hull

Dancefloor ditzes

I was at our school disco with my best friend when my
fave song came on. We got so excited we ran towards
the dancefloor, only for my friend to trip and go flying,
dragging me down with her! The embarrassing thing
was that, while she was wearing jeans, I was wearing
my new skirt, which flew up flashing my knickers to
everyone! The worst part was that my ex-boyfriend saw
and spent the entire night pointing at me and laughing
about it with his horrible mates!

Charlotte, Brighton

Oops… I did it again!

My best mates were round at mine and we were all
messing about in my room, singing. We were just getting
to the chorus of one song, so I turned the radio up full
blast and really belted it out. Suddenly, my brother burst
in and took a photo of us! I was so embarrassed! He's
been blackmailing me with it ever since!

Kate, by email

Window pain

On the way back from a school trip, we stopped at a service station. I was absolutely desperate for the loo, so I shoved my way off the coach and towards the entrance. Trouble was, the automatic doors wouldn't open, no matter how much I jumped up and down in front of them. Eventually, I realised I was just in front of a window and the doors were actually around on another side of the building! People inside were staring at me like I was crazy and my class, and even our teacher, were in hysterics!

Julia, Cambridge

● ●

How alarming!

I was at a burger bar with my mates and they sent me to get some more napkins. I went to the toilet first and was about to go back out the same way I'd come in, when I saw another door. I went through that one, and didn't realise it was a fire exit! The alarm started to go off and all my friends saw me do it. The shame!

Sally, Islington

4

Total loo-nacy!

I was in the girls' toilets at school when, for a laugh,
I decided to climb on top of the loo and yell "Boo!" at my
mate in the next cubicle. But, as I balanced all my weight
on one foot, the seat cracked and my foot went down into
the bowl. My shoe got wedged there and I freaked out,
so my mate had to help me pull it free, watched by a
crowd of hysterical girls. I still get teased about it now!

Melissa, Glamorgan

A crying shame

It was a gorgeous sunny day, so my mates and I went outside and decided to play hide and seek, for a laugh. I sneaked behind a wall – not the cleverest hiding place – so, when I heard the seeker get closer, I knew I had no chance. I leaped up and yelled, "Raaa!", waving my arms around. Only it wasn't my mate, it was a little girl, who was so scared she burst out crying. I felt so awful about it!

Chloe, Brighton

Bin raider

My mum managed to get me and a few friends tickets to a big pop gig, and we went for burgers on the way to the show. I had my ticket out while we were sat eating and, unfortunately, when I went to put my rubbish in the bin afterwards, I accidentally threw it away, too! There was no way I was going to miss the gig, and so I started to rummage through the bin until I found it. My mates disowned me within about five seconds and everyone else must have thought I looked like a tramp! At least the band were worth all the shame, I guess!

Lauren, Penrith

Holding on

I was watching TV with my friend and we were both
in a silly, giggly mood. She said something really funny
and I collapsed in hysterics. I'd been starting to feel like
I needed the toilet and was horrified when I realised I *had*
actually wet myself a bit! Most stupid of all, though, I told
my mate, who's now never gonna let me forget about it!

Matilda, London

A bit of a boob

My friend Tamzin and I had just walked past a bra shop
and were talking about it on our way home. I was so
involved in the conversation that I didn't notice a man
walking past us as I said, in a very loud voice, "I'd go in
and ask if they had any bras for small breasts!" The man
gave us a really strange look and I felt so embarrassed
I walked slap-bang into a wall!

May, Leeds

Piggy palava

I was at a farm with my best mate and it was a really rainy day. We were sat on the fence by where the pigs were, looking at them rolling around in the mud. My mum took a pic of us but, just as the camera snapped, I slipped and fell into the pig pen! I was covered in pig poo and muddy sludge! What made it worse was that my mum kept on taking photos as I struggled!

Louisa, East Sussex

Mobile mishap

I got a really expensive phone for my birthday and showed it off to all my mates while I was out shopping. As I was talking, one of the girls grabbed it and started messing around. As I went to snatch it back from her, it slipped out of her hand and flew through the air, hitting a complete stranger on the head before falling on the pavement and shattering! Mum wasn't too happy when I explained how it had got broken!

Ella, London

Roll up, roll up!

I had a sleepover at my house with my two best friends. One girl was running late as usual so, getting a bit bored as we waited for her to turn up, we began to muck around, putting my mum's knickers and bras on over our clothes and stuffing the cups with loo roll. The doorbell rang and, thinking it was our mate, we ran to answer it – only to find it was our ultra-cute paperboy instead!

Laura and Harley, by email

Sleeptalkin'

It was my friend's party sleepover, and I spent hours going on about my new boyfriend, Tyler. When I woke up the next morning, all my friends started saying, "Oh, Tyler, I love your new socks!" and making kissing noises. I thought they where teasing me about going on about him so much, but later I found out that I'd been talking in my sleep and I'd said "Oh, Tyler, I love your new socks…" But what made it worse was that my mate had recorded it on her phone and she showed it to Tyler! My face just went scarlet!

Juliette, Wirral

Ringtone moan

I was shopping with a friend and, as we waited to get served in a sweetshop, a mobile phone began to ring. It went on for ages and got really irritating, My mate and I started huffing, hoping its owner would take the hint, then she said, in a loud, sarky voice, "Answer it already!" That's when I realised it was my phone – I'd forgotten that I'd changed the ringtone! We had to queue for ages with people glaring at us before we could make a swift exit!

Freya, Inverness

Bra-vo!

I recently went shopping with my friend to look for our first-ever bras. As a joke, I picked up the biggest bra I could find and said, "I think this one is a bit small for me!" I started dancing around with it 'til I noticed the shop assistant giving me disapproving looks. Embarrassed, I went to put it back but walked straight into a shop dummy, knocking it off its stand!

Anna, by email

Ruby slippers, red face

I'd seen a gorgeous pair of red shoes and, thinking they'd impress everyone, I bought them to wear out that evening. Spotting my crush, I put on my best strut and walked past him and his mates. To my embarrassment, one of his friends shouted, "Dorothy, eat your heart out!" and then started to sing "We're off to see the wizard, the wonderful Wizard Of Oz!" at the top of his voice. Definitely not the reaction I'd hoped for!

Taylor, Devon

Can't top this!

I was trying on some clothes in a shop changing room when I noticed a really nice top that had been left in the cubicle opposite. I put it on and came out for a better look in the mirror. I was wondering whether or not to buy it, when a woman in just her bra tapped me on the shoulder and said, "Excuse me, that's actually *my* top!" I was so embarrassed I couldn't get it off quick enough!

Kaley, Chadderton

A model idiot

I found a gorgeous prom dress in a charity shop and tried it on. It was so cool I started striking model poses – then realised the sales assistant was behind me, trying not to laugh. I'd been admiring myself for so long, she'd come in to check if I was OK!

mizz **fan, by email**

Flying low

I was walking along listening to my MP3, when a group of foreign tourists stopped me and started talking to me. I took my earphones out to hear them but I couldn't understand what they were saying. It wasn't 'til they started pointing that I realised they'd stopped me to tell my flies were undone! To make it worse, loads of people had come over to see what all the fuss was about!

Kirk Franklin fan, Buckinghamshire

Lip slip

I was shopping with my mates and we were looking at lipsticks. I didn't know whether or not one of the shades suited me so I decided to try it on. I held it up to my lips but slipped and completely missed, smudging it all over my chin! My friends were doubled-up in laughter.

Lizzie, Crewe

Gift gaffe

I threw a birthday party a few years ago, and one of my mates bought me a fab silky dress. I loved it, and wore it when I went into town to meet her and the girls the following week. I got some strange looks walking to meet them, and when I turned up my mate was in fits of giggles. The dress was actually a nightie! Argh!

Alice, by email

Tongs gone wrong

My bro was inviting some cute mates over to our family barbecue, so I wanted to look my best. I saw a pic of Ashlee Simpson with fab wavy 'do, so I borrowed a pal's curling tongs to style my hair the same. It all went fine until, somehow, I managed to get them tangled up in my locks! I ran out into the garden to look for my mum to help me unravel it. She did, but not 'til everyone – including my bro's hottie friends – had a good laugh at me!

Gem, by email

Vintage style

I was going shopping so I asked my mates' advice on where to go. They told me about a cool new shop that had opened, so I went there. The first thing I noticed was that all the customers in there were quite old, but I decided to check it out anyway. A random man then came up to me and said, "Are you looking for your granny?" I ran out mortified, only to find two of my friends outside in absolute hysterics!

Samantha, Suffolk

Tan-tastic

After coming back from a party, I went into my mum's room to get some make-up remover. I found what I thought were cleansing wipes, and scrubbed my face clean with them. The next morning, I woke up to find I was bright orange – they had actually been tanning wipes and the colour had gone on streaky, too! Now I always make sure I read the label!

Pete Wentz fan, by email

Sticky pins

I was running late for a shopping trip with my mates and had just got out of the bath. I sat down to moisturise my legs on the bed and was rushing to get them done quickly. As I walked down the stairs, my mum burst out laughing. An ad leaflet from one of my magazines had stuck to the leg I was moisturising! At least I didn't go out like that!

Jen, Oxford

Baby blush

My mum treated me to a day out shopping for clothes, and I was so excited to try on all the latest fashions. I found the most amazing pair of jeans and ran straight to the till to pay for them. The lady behind the counter looked at me strangely and asked if I realised that I had picked up maternity wear. I could feel everyone in the queue was staring and I went bright red. So embarrassing!

Barbara, Norwich

Thanks, pal!

For my birthday, my friend bought me a gift card for a big chemists' chain, so I had a big splurge on bath and beauty products. But, as I handed over my card, the shop assistant said there was no money on it! I felt so embarrassed I spent ages putting all the products back on to the shelves before I felt able to leave. So much for friends and their "thoughtful" pressies!

Mizzie, Bradford

. . . .

What a rip-off!

I went shopping with my mate and, for a laugh, we were picking up the worst clothes we could find. I grabbed this awful miniskirt off a display and was flaunting it in front of her in the middle of the shop. Then, as I swung round laughing, it got caught on a rail and it ripped in two! We haven't been allowed back in the shop since.

Penny, Windsor

Fashion flops 'n' beauty blunders

Squeezy does it...

Out shopping with my mates, I found the perfect dress,
but not in my size. So, I tried the next one down, thinking
I could squeeze into it. I got it on – just about – only to find
I couldn't get it back off again! None of my mates could
budge it either, without it feeling like it would tear, so I had
to call a shop assistant. I stood in the changing room in
just my undies for ages while she peeled it off me!

Molly, Margate

Shoe shenanigans

I was in a shoe shop with my friend and, as we browsed, we were laughing at some of the shoes they had on sale, saying how ugly they were. I spotted a really awful pair and held them up, sneering, "Eww... Gross!" Then I noticed my boyfriend's mum queuing for the tills, holding an identical pair! And yes, she'd heard everything I'd said and didn't look happy!

Hilary, Derby

DIY drama

I was sleeping over at my mate's house and she was telling me about a homemade facepack she'd tried the night before. She still had some left over and told me I should give it a go. About a minute after I put it on, my skin began to tingle – she said that just meant it was working. Then, when I rinsed it off, my face was covered in sore, red blotches! "That happened to me, too," she said. I asked why on earth she'd let me use it and she said, "I just thought your skin would be OK." Like, duh!

Becca, Northampton

Why the red face?

Have you ever wanted the ground to open up and swallow you whole? If the answer is yes, you're probably wondering why you get so embarrassed. People can feel red-faced for all kinds of reasons but here's why you might get flustered…

Feeling silly

If you think back to all the times when you've been embarrassed, you'll see that they all stem from the same thing – doing something that you think seems silly or funny to others. Sticking out from the crowd for any reason can be cringeworthy at the best of times – which is probably why you end up feeling so uncomfortable!

A confidence crisis

When you have a slip-up, it can knock your confidence, which causes a serious attack of the blushes. This kind of shyness or lack of assurance tends to strike in certain kinds of social situations – like when you're meeting someone new, striking up a conversation with someone you feel attracted to or, in this case, when you feel daft.

All eyes on you

Unless you're a born performer, being the centre of attention can be plain awkward. Doing anything out of the ordinary will capture the attention of some, or even many people which may even include your crush! Feeling like you're in the spotlight can be daunting and will make you blush.

Body signs

The feelings of embarrassment are tricky to escape as they often show up on your body! If you feel instantly uncomfortable, it's likely that your heart rate will go up and you'll be breathing quicker than usual. When this happens, blood rushes to our muscles and some of it goes to our face. This is why you turn tomato red! These reactions are completely normal, so don't worry. It really does happen to everyone!

What to do...

If you find yourself in an embarrassing position, don't run away and hide! While you may want to dash off in the opposite direction or go dive under your duvet for quite possibly the rest of your life, neither is actually a do-able option. Blushing with embarrassment isn't anything to be ashamed of and the feelings will pass. Promise! If you need more help, turn to p48 for our top tips on beating the blushes…

Knock me flat!

Chatting to a friend as I walked out of the school gates, I wasn't paying attention to what was going on around me. I stepped off the pavement to cross the road to the bus stop and, next thing I knew, I was lying flat out on the ground! My maths teacher, who rides a bike to school, had knocked me over! I was totally unhurt, but I've never been so embarrassed!

Sally, Harlow

Écoutez!

Before our French listening exam, our teacher tested out the tape machine, to check that everyone could hear it OK. Pressing play, she said that if anyone couldn't make out what was being said, to put up their hand. Filling in the front of my paper, I put my hand up, but when I looked around I realised I was the only one in the whole year who'd raised their hand! I haven't lived it down since and my friends still call me Cloth Ears!

Sarah, Kent

Nap time

On the way back from our school trip, I felt very tired. We still had a good way to go before we got home, so I decided to take a little nap. I woke up with a jolt to realise that, in my sleep, I'd leaned up against the girl in the seat next to mine and dribbled all down her new top. She'd angrily nudged me awake and didn't forgive me for ages!

Charlie, Leeds

Tummy turmoil

It was the day of my Spanish oral exam and I was really nervous. When it got to my turn, I was so scared I felt sick and my stomach started rumbling really loudly. As I took my seat next to the examiner's desk, she pressed record on the tape machine. I opened my mouth to start my speech but the only thing that came out was a huge burp! She had to rewind the tape and start it again!

Embarrassed *mizz* reader, Leeds

. . . .

What a display!

After finishing an exam early and checking it through, I put my hand up to leave the hall. My teacher nodded for me to go and I got up as quietly as I could so that I didn't disturb the people still working. Creeping around the other desks, I'd almost reached the door when I tripped over the leg of a display stand, falling over and whacking another student in the head! Poor thing, she didn't know what had hit her!

Bea, Lincoln

Chair one minute, gone the next!

Bored in an IT class, I amused myself by swivelling on my chair. As I did so, my friend's coat got caught in the seat and ripped. As if this wasn't bad enough, the tangle caused the chair to topple over and I fell headfirst on to the floor! Everyone laughed except my teacher, who insisted that I go to see the school nurse to make sure I didn't have concussion. Now I always sit still in my seat!

Emily, Hampshire

Smelly stare-out

At lunchtime one day, my mates and I decided, for some silly reason, to have a staring contest. I was doing really well against my best mate but then I accidentally let out the biggest fart ever. All my friends burst out laughing and I went beetroot with shame! I didn't win either!

Jen, Dorset

Pond panic

One day at school, we spent our biology lesson pond-dipping and, spotting something potentially interesting in the middle of the pond, I stepped nearer to the edge to get a better look. As I tried to make out what it was, two boys play-fighting behind me knocked me over into the water. My mate tried to help but she slipped, too and we both came out dripping wet. Gross!

Peta, West Felton

Sick of chocolate

At school, one of my best mates brought in some leftover chocolate cake, home-made by her mum. I ate loads before we went into our first lesson and started to feel queasy during the class – and I got steadily worse as it went on. I must have gone a bit green as my teacher asked if I was OK. And, as she did, I jumped up to run out to the loo. Too bad I didn't make it – I threw up on her shoes! I haven't had chocolate or cake since then.

Christine, Bexley

Canteen calamity

In the school canteen one lunchtime, I got up to take my tray of dirty crockery and cutlery to the little hatch to be washed. The floor was wet and I slipped on it, and the leftover food came flying off my plate and hit a dinner lady who's known for being grumpy. She was so annoyed she told the head I'd done it on purpose – it took a lot of explaining to convince him it had been an accident!

Louisa, Devon

Water disaster!

In one of my exams I was really thirsty, so I put my hand up for some water – and then managed to spill half of it all over my answer sheet. I panicked as all the ink started smudging, and tried to blot the page as best I could with my school jumper. In the end, I had to draw a big circle around the blotchy mess and write an apology to the examiner! Needless to say, I didn't get a good grade.

Helen, Cardiff

Shower of shame

On a school trip, I took a shower before lunch. I came out in my towel, dripping wet, but couldn't find any of my mates in our dorm. I saw a note saying that they were in the hall. I stepped out, still in my towel, to look for them, only to find all the teachers and the rest of the class waiting there. My friends still talk about it now!

Daisy, Surrey

Sticky situation

I was in the same science class as my crush and the teacher had left the room to get some books. One of my friends asked to borrow my big glue-stick so I threw it to her, but, just as I did, my crush stood up and it hit him in the face! When he took his hand away, he had a massive red mark on his cheek – he hasn't spoken to me since!

Abi, Haywards Heath

Bottle it up

Sitting with my mates as we waited for afternoon registration, I couldn't find my bottle of water. Suddenly, I spotted it on the teacher's desk and figured a mate had put it there for a laugh, so I grabbed it and took a big swig from it. The teacher came in, saw me with it, and asked what I thought I was doing, drinking her water. "It's *mine*," I said, a bit too cheekily, and then my bezzie pointed out my empty water bottle in the bin, where I'd put it! I got detention for trying to be smart!

Georgia, Brighton

Ever bin shamed?

I was walking down the corridor at school when suddenly I saw my crush walking towards me. I was trying to act cool, so I flipped my hair. As I was doing it, I tripped over my own feet and landed in a rubbish bin that was brim-full of leftovers from lunchtime. Argh!

Lilly, St Helens

Marked for mirth

I was doing my geography coursework in town, with my brother helping me to log the traffic near the shopping centre. He'd say what he was seeing and I'd tick it off with a big marker pen. Afterwards, we went to grab a burger and a soft drink, and I noticed I was getting funny looks. But it wasn't 'til I got home that I realised why! I looked in the mirror and saw I had huge black splodges from the marker all down my face! My bro had thought it would be funny not to tell me! Grrr…

Louise, Marlow

Choir cringe

Recently, our school choir did a performance in front of all the pupils and teachers. I'd been asked to sing a solo and was so nervous! When I took a breath and went forward to sing, my legs went weak and I fell off the stage, almost knocking a teacher over in the process. Everyone laughed and my choir teacher hasn't asked me to sing on my own again!

Sammi, Leicester

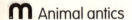

Chewed 'do!

I went on a trip to the zoo with my family and I couldn't wait to see the donkeys in Pets' Corner, as they're my favourite animals. When we got to see them, one of the zookeepers said I could go in and stroke them. I was so chuffed until one of them started chewing on my bunches! I lost a lot of hair that day!

Beth, Monmouth

Pup-pee

One day, I was with my mate when I saw my neighbour's fit son out walking his dog. I'd been going on to her about how gorge he was, so she suggested we should go and say hi to him. Plucking up the courage, I started walking towards him, but his dog came bounding up to me before I got there. I bent down to stroke him but, instead of letting me fuss over him, he stopped, peed down my leg and then ran off! I was so humiliated, I felt like crying!

Caroline, Shropshire

Horsing around

I was at the stables with my friend and was petting her horse when I felt something tug at the hem of my dress. I looked down to see another horse snuffling its nose up under it! I screamed and stumbled backwards, slipping on a pile of horse poo and collapsing on to a massive pile of hay bales! At least it was a soft landing!

***mizz* fan, Gloucester**

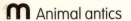
Hungry hammy

My cousin and his lush mate were at my house one day and we were playing with my hamster. I asked his friend to look after it while I went to clean the cage out but, when I came back, he looked really annoyed. I asked him what was wrong, and he showed me a massive hole in the sleeve of his jumper. My hamster had gnawed straight through it! The worst thing was, it was a brand new jumper he'd been given for his birthday the day before!

Catherine, Exeter

Catfight

I was watching a DVD with my crush when his cat came in and jumped on to my lap. I'm not really a cat fan but I thought it'd look good if I bonded with his pet, so I started stroking it. All of a sudden, its claws came out and dug into my arm! I screamed and the cat ran away, and if that wasn't embarrassing enough, the wound bled all over the cream sofa! I haven't been invited back since!

Lowri, Aberystwyth

Squ-eeek!

I was at my friend's house, chilling out and listening to some music, when I heard something rustling next to me. I lifted up the cushion, and saw a huge rat tail sticking out! I screamed and ran out of the room, with my friend dashing after me to find out what was wrong. In a right state, I said she had a rodent problem. She started giggling and dragged me back in, then showed me her bro's big cage of actually quite cute pet rats! I felt so stupid!

Danni, London

Dog-gone!

When my dad and I went to our local farmer's market, we took our Staffy bull terrier along for a walk. Suddenly, she yanked the lead out of my hand and ran off. By the time we caught up with, her she'd jumped up on one of the cake stalls and was pigging out!

Kelly, Dorset

Monkeying around

On a school trip to the zoo, my class was looking around the monkey house. When my friend pointed out a monkey hiding in the hay, I couldn't see it. Suddenly it charged towards me, causing me to scream like a mad thing. Everyone turned round and I went bright red!

Tina, Wrexham

Dragged through a hedge

My uncle was ill one day and asked me to walk his dog, Casey. I took her to the park and started throwing a stick for her. I noticed a group of cute boys watching me from the swings, so I picked the stick up and threw it extra hard. It landed in a clump of hedges and Casey chased after it. I waited a while but she didn't return, so, in the end, I had to go in after her. When I finally dragged her out, I had twigs in my hair and mud all over me. All the boys laughed, and I was left wishing I'd just stayed in the hedge!

Katie, Winchester

Showdown!

Every year, my village holds a pet show to raise money for charity. Last year, I decided to take my rabbit along and enter her into it. I was getting really nervous because it was almost my turn. Finally, the judges came to my table, but just as they were about to pick her up, she leaped off the table and hopped away! Everyone in the hall started chasing her, causing absolute chaos! Dogs were barking, and people were tripping over everywhere, it was so cringey! Needless to say, I didn't win a prize!

Rebecca, Cornwall

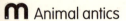

Doggie drama

I was in the park playing on the swings with my sister, when I saw a dog running towards me. I started getting really nervous because it was running really fast and barking. I screamed and stood on the seat of the swing to get away from it. It wasn't 'til it started licking my feet that I realised how much I'd overreacted, with my sis and the owner laughing about what a wimp I was!

Jo, Manchester

Kitty commotion

I was at my crush's house, playing with his cat, when he went into the kitchen to get a drink. Suddenly his cat started choking and I didn't know what to do! I panicked and screamed, "Oh my god, your cat's dying!" He came running in, terrified, and then, to my surprise, burst out laughing. Not being a cat owner, I didn't realise it was only coughing up a fur ball! I felt like such an idiot!

Sarah, East Sussex

Poo shoe

I went on a school trip to a local farm last term. I was looking at all the animals with my crush and having a laugh when we came across a horse. I was bragging about how much I knew about horses when it backed towards me and did a poo – which landed right on my shoe! My crush went red, stumbled off and didn't speak to me for the rest of the day. And my mate got her mobile out and filmed me stood in a steaming pile of manure!

Samantha, Winchester

Losing my grip!

I was at my mate's house looking at her two-week-old puppies – they were so small and cute! I picked one up but accidentally dropped it when it wriggled in my hands, and it landed in some wee that the other pups had done and began to whimper! My mate's mum was not pleased and I haven't been invited back since.

Helena, Bradford

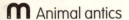

Horsing around

I love horses and recently signed up for riding lessons so I could spend more time at my local stables. After I'd been doing it for a while, my instructor told us that we'd be trying some simple jumps. I got on my horse and began riding. When we got to the fence, though, my horse tripped, sending me flying through the air. My boot fell off and I landed face-down in the mud. So gross!

Mizz fan, Brentwood

In the doghouse

I went round to my mate's house and we were playing in the garden with her dog. He was going completely mad and started chasing me, pulling and pulling at my trousers until they came down! What was worse was that my mate's lush bro saw everything, including the pair of pink Barbie knickers I was wearing! How embarrassing!

Helena, Weymouth

Cat-astrophic!

I went round to my friend's house one morning to get a lift to school. As I was sat on the sofa waiting for her to finish getting ready, her cat came and sat on my lap. Then, as I stroked it, it weed on me! I knew I wouldn't be able to get back into my own house to change, and we didn't want to be late for school anyway. So, although I did my best to clean the wee-patch off the skirt, I couldn't totally get rid of the smell! Bleugh!

Becca, Northampton

Beat the blushes!

If you find yourself in a beetroot-face situation, don't panic – here's our five-step guide for bustin' the blush!

Smile

So what if you were trying on a fleece in a shop and got your hair caught up in the zip? So what if the snotty assistant had to help you untangle it? Don't cringe indefinitely, just smile at her and laugh it off. Bet she's seen it all before!

While it may be easier said than done, laughing it off is most definitely the best thing you can do. You've gotta giggle about it – because when you laugh, the world will laugh with you. And, let's face it, there really is nothing more attractive than a girl who looks like she knows how to have fun.

Act up

If you trip over your words when you try to talk to the cute boy in your maths class, or find yourself wearing the exact same outfit as your best galpal, don't stress, just stand tall and do as we do. Ask yourself what your favourite movie star would do. For real! If ever we find ourselves in a potential blush-like situation, we ask, "What would Amanda Bynes do?"

If she turned up to a celeb party wearing the same outfit as her co-star, we bet she'd simply smile and brush off any feelings of embarrassment, pronto. So, make like your fave movie star, and act confident, no matter what the situation. That way you'll get away with practically anything!

Be silly

Don't take yourself too seriously. OK, so you've walked into class and realised that the buttons on your blouse have come undone, exposing your bra. Instead of running in the opposite direction, give your classmates a cheeky wink and do a silly dance. Oh, and then button up, obviously!

Love yourself up

If you're still cringing from the shame of letting out a bottom burp in front of your best bud and her family – quit it!

Beating yourself up about it is gonna get you nowhere, so just forget about it! Instead, collect compliments – write 'em down in a cute lil' journal and you can flick back to it any time you need to remind yourself of how totally fabulous you are.

Think positive!

If, after an embarrassing incident, you're thinking: "What a total idiot! OMG, I'm so dumb!" flick your negative thinking switch to positive and say this instead. "It could have turned out a whole lot worse – it's really not such a big deal!"

The drinks are on him!

My crush's dad is a builder and my folks hired him to resurface our driveway. As it was the school hols, my crush was helping him, so I made sure I looked my best whenever I went outside. Dressed my cutest skirt and heels, I took them out a tray of drinks, but tripped over some rubble and went flying. My crush was absolutely soaked in lemonade, and he told all his mates back at school!

Mizz fan, Ireland

Brotherly banter

I was on my first date with my new boyfriend and we were having a great time. We were walking down the road with our arms around each other when, with no warning, my brother appeared from behind a bush, wolf whistling. When I ignored him, he started singing *Love Is In The Air* at the top of his voice! My lad got all embarrassed and scarpered, leaving me to walk home on my own!

Edel, Whitehead

Give us a hand

One day I was out with my boyfriend and we were walking along, hand in hand. I noticed a couple of girls I knew across the street, so I went to go and talk to them. When I came back over to I my boyfriend, I grabbed his hand and said, "Ready to go, babe?" when I realised it wasn't him at all! My boyfriend couldn't stop laughing at the thought of me grabbing a complete stranger!

Laura, Whitehead

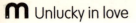

Snack attack

I was in the cinema with my new boyfriend and needed to go to the loo. When I came back, I sat down and reached over to get some popcorn. It wasn't 'til I looked up that I realised I was in completely the wrong seat trying to grab popcorn from a random boy! I ran out of the auditorium and ended up waiting 'til the film finished for my boyfriend to come out!

Red-faced reader, Wokingham

Nerd alert!

I'd been moaning about not having a boyfriend, so my friend set me up on a blind date. I was waiting outside the cinema for him, when the biggest geek in school turned up. I tried to avoid him as I didn't want my date to think I was a geek, too. To my horror, though, he came straight up to me and said, "Hi, Alice, I'm your date!"

Alice, Derbyshire

Deuce dunce

I was on a date with a sports-obsessed lad, and he was going on about Roger Federer, his idol. I was trying my hardest to sound interested and said, "Yeah, I guess he's OK, but I'm not really into football." He was so shocked he almost choked on his lunch and told me, very coldly, "He's a tennis player, actually. He's won Wimbledon." And nope, never asked me on another date!

Julia, Poole

• •

Pucker up!

I was at my crush's house when he asked me if I wanted a drink. I said yes, so he went to get me one, and, thinking that he might try and kiss me that evening, I took the opportunity to mime out and practice what I'd do just in case he did make a move. It would have been fine if he hadn't walked straight back in to ask which flavour squash I'd prefer! Oh dear…

Aimee, Huddersfield

Thr-ill ride

My crush had invited me to go to a theme park with him and his family. We were having such a laugh until he suggested going on the biggest rollercoaster there. Not wanting to look like a wimp, I pretended I'd enjoyed it. Thinking I was having fun, he made me go on it three more times in a row. I felt so ill afterwards that I had to run to the toilet to be sick!

Mary, Scarborough

Textaholic

In class, I sent my bezzie a text saying how hot my crush was. Her phone beeped loudly and, as we're meant to switch them off during lessons, our teacher made her bring it up to the front of the class, then read the text out loud. This included my name, as I shouldn't have been texting, either! I was so ashamed I wanted to crawl off, and my crush was so annoyed at being shown up like that.

Orlando Bloom fan, Whitby

A bum deal!

When I went swimming with my boyfriend and his mates the lifeguards held a competition to see who could make the biggest splash. My boyfriend did a great bomb-jump but, when he started climbing out of the pool, his trunks had slipped, giving him a really bad "builder's bum". Everyone starting cheering and, thinking he'd won, he came up and gave me a massive hug. It wasn't 'til I whispered 'Everyone saw your bum!' that he twigged!

Gabz, Kent

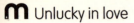
Camping catastrophe

I was on a camping holiday and had been flirting all week with a couple of fit lads staying in a tent near ours. On the last night, I walked back from the toilet block and got into bed. I suddenly felt something against my leg, so I shone my torch on it to see one of the fit boys! I'd climbed into the wrong tent by mistake!

Ellan, Manchester

Crush blush

I was standing with my best boy mate outside our classroom, when he accused me of fancying his best friend. I asked who'd told him, thinking he already knew, and he said he'd just been guessing. Just as I was pleading with him not to tell anyone, he started laughing. I turned around to see my crush standing right behind me - he'd heard the whole conversation!

CuteNGawjuz, by email

Locker love

I'd fancied this boy for ages and, last Valentine's Day, I finally plucked up the courage to send him a card. I snuck into the classroom before school and slid it under the door of his locker. I was really nervous all first period because I couldn't wait for him to open his locker and find it. Imagine my embarrassment when I saw another boy opening and reading it! I'd only slipped it into the wrong locker by mistake!

Nicola, Wolverhampton

Crisp cringe

My best mate and I were at our school disco and, feeling peckish, we went to get a drink and some crisps from the tuck shop. Later on in the night, a really cute boy asked me to dance. Everything was going great until he moved in for a kiss. Suddenly he pulled this really weird face. It wasn't 'til I opened my mouth to ask what was wrong that I noticed my disgusting cheese and onion breath! I didn't get snogged, obviously!

Alexa, Nottingham

I'm not wall right

My mates, including my crush, and I went over to the park to chill out. We decided to climb over a wall as a short-cut and they all managed it easily. I'd never been good at climbing but I wanted to show off in front of my crush, so I just went for it. Everyone was watching as my foot slipped, and I slammed down on the wall, landing right between my legs! I was in so much pain, but had to keep a brave face to avoid any further embarrassment.

Stephanie, by email

Spaghett-itch

My new boyfriend was babysitting his lil' bro and invited me over to keep him company. When I arrived, he was cooking spaghetti in sauce – and I didn't have the heart to tell him I have a mild allergy to mushrooms. We started eating, and although I picked out all the mushrooms, they'd obviously seeped into the sauce. I could feel myself getting really flushed. My face was getting itchy and a rash began to develop on my neck. My boyfriend freaked out, and in the end, I had to call my mum to fetch me home!

Louise, Loughborough

• • • • • • • • • • • • • • • • • • • •

Say cheese!

I was video-calling a really cute lad on my webcam, and he was pulling funny faces to make me laugh. Unfortunately, while I was laughing, my web cam froze, and I looked like I was screaming in a really freaky way! He told everyone at my school the next day – blush-a-rama!

Aoife, Cork

54

Locker laughter

At a swimming gala, my friend and I decided to have a laugh and see if we could fit in the lockers. She managed it, so then I tried. After wedging myself in I realised I was completely stuck! As I struggled to wriggle my way out, an "audience" gathered round, laughing hysterically. My mum and my entire swimming team ended up trying to pull me free, almost dislocating my arm!

Sammy, by email

Run away!

My auntie is a personal trainer and always encouraging me to exercise. Last weekend, she invited me over to show off some new gym equipment she'd bought. When I got there, I was mortified to find my cousin was there too, with all his fit mates. Nervously, I started to jog on the treadmill. Just as I was getting into it, my cousin's friend walked past and grinned at me. I tried to smile back, but I was so distracted that I forgot to keep running! I lost my footing and slid backwards, landing flat on my bum. It was quite badly bruised, but not as much as my pride!

Lauren, Surrey

Eye eye!

I'd just bought the latest must-have mascara, and thought I'd wear it to school and bat my lashes as my crush. This turned out to be a huge mistake! I started to feel a bit weird, then one of my mates said, "Oh my god – what's wrong with your eyes?" I went into the bathroom and looked in the mirror and saw my eyes were all red and puffy. I'd obviously had a bad reaction to the make-up!

Scissor Sisters fan, London

You're sacked!

Trust me to forget my PE kit on our school sports day, but the teacher said I could do the sack race in my school dress. I said OK, and did fine until halfway through the race – when I fell over. I heard the crowd laughing their heads off, and thought it was just about me tripping. But, after it was all over, I found out the real reason – my skirt had flipped up and I'd flashed my hideous heart-patterned red knickers everyone in the crowd!

Nia, Wales

Bunch of drips!

Deciding we should really do more exercise, my mates and I signed up for the school swimming team and entered a gala. To our shock, we won and, after a lot of celebrating by the pool, we went back to the changing rooms to get dry and dressed – only to find that all our clothes were missing! Our teacher made us wear some really old clothes from the PE cupboard and I had to walk the whole way home in gross, smelly boy-shorts!

McFly fan, Surrey

Header!

One week we had an important netball match against
another girls' school – traditionally our biggest rivals.
As we started playing, one of my mates passed the ball
to me. I got scared when one of players from the other
team tried to stop me throwing it and, in a panic, I just
threw it, not looking where it was going. It headed
straight for the coach and hit her in the face! She had
a bruised nose for a week afterwards!

Jenny, Kent

Lifesaving lunacy

At the end of our swimming lesson, we were allowed
some free time in the pool to play around. I was sitting
at the side of the pool when I noticed one of the boys
was struggling in the water. Thinking he was drowning,
I dived in and tried to save him. When I came up for air,
he was staring at me like I was crazy – it turned out he'd
just been messing around with his mates and everyone
in my class was laughing at me!

Helen, Shropshire

Swimming slip-up

I'd gone to my swimming class and couldn't wait to get started. At our local pool, they have music playing and I was dancing away and showing off in front of my mates. As I was spinning around, I lost my footing and slipped headfirst into the pool. All my mates laughed and my teacher looked horrified! I won't be showing off like that again in a hurry…

Polly, Sussex

Beware of the bat!

I was in PE and we were playing rounders. I really liked this lush boy in my class, so I thought I'd try to catch his eye by swinging the bat behind me to hit the ball hard – only to smack him right in the head. It left him with a massive, sore bump and he told all his friends who now laugh at me at every opportunity!

Kay, by email

Fallin' for you

For our school sports day, me and my mate, Karen, ran the three-legged race. As we're both really clumsy, we decided it would be better if we walked rather than ran. However, when I saw everyone else beating us I decided maybe we should speed up. Of course, telling Karen would have been a good idea as she kept walking, and the pair of us fell over on to the floor. I've seen the photos people took and we looked even stupider than we felt!

Ellen, Ireland

Fancy flop

There's a boy I really like in my swimming class, and I decided to try and get his attention by doing my best dive into the deep end. But, as I was about to dive in, I slipped and ended up doing a huge belly flop and splashing into the water really loudly. As well as laughing at me, he and his mates even did impressions. Nice!

Charlotte, Scunthorpe

T-shirt trauma

Normally in gym class I wear my leotard with a T-shirt and shorts over the top but, one particularly sunny day, I just wore shorts and a T-shirt to try and stay cool. During the class I felt boiling hot, so I whipped off my tee, thinking my leotard was underneath as usual. I did remember it wasn't, but not before I'd flashed my entire class!

Samrana, Liverpool

Bad move!

In our PE lesson, we had to grab a partner so I paired up with my bezzie. We got some apparatus set up and had to climb up and down it. I was messing about and being silly and decided to climb diagonally, then got stuck in the apparatus and couldn't move! My teacher had to help me down and I got in lots of trouble. So embarrassing!

Emily, Nottingham

Pack it in!

I was late for school and in a massive rush, so I had to pack my PE kit double-quick. I'd just got on to the bus when I realised everyone was laughing. I wasn't sure why but then looked outside and saw my mum running toward the bus waving my gym pants around shouting, "You've forgotten your knickers!" I was so mortified!

Emma, Lowestoft

Eating sand

One day, in a PE lesson, we had a long-jump contest and,
being really competitive, I was determined to win. So,
I launched myself at top speed towards the sand. As
I looked over to check everyone was watching, I slipped
and face-planted into the sand. As I sat up covered in the
stuff, everyone was laughing like crazy. Argh!

Molly, Manchester

Hurdles horror

We were doing athletics at school and trying out the hurdles. I was nervous, because they seemed really high and close together, so I just went for it. I cleared the first one fine, then totally misjudged the next one and went crashing into it. The school had to ring an ambulance 'cause they thought I'd broken my ankle
– luckily for me it was only sprained!

Louisa, Horsham

· ·

Football fever

I've always been a bit of a tomboy and, when the lads from school invited me to play football, I couldn't wait to get on the pitch and show off my skills. I was doing really well 'til I attempted a kick for goal. I slipped and slid all the way into the goal mouth, knocking the keeper flying in the process! Luckily, the lads thought it was hilarious, so I've really bonded with them now!

Penny, Glasgow

Friends' faux pas

When something embarrassing happens to another person, say, a mate, your natural reaction is to point and laugh. It's harsh but true – people like to have a giggle at the misfortunes of others, especially in seemingly funny situations. The class bully accidentally steps in a giant puddle, you catch your bezzie and her lad clashing noses when they kiss – it's funny, right? But what happens when something really mortifying happens to a pal – do you laugh at their expense or do you support them through the crisis? Follow our simple guide…

1 Judge the situation

Is it something she'll be laughing at in two hours' time, or will she be crying herself to sleep over it for the next week? Ask yourself how you'd feel if it happened to you, and whether it'd make it 10 times worse if all your mates poked fun as well.

2 Be honest

If your friend has fallen down a flight of steps in front of the whole school, lying to her that no one noticed isn't gonna help. The whole world clearly just saw her mishap and there's no denying it. Instead, acknowledge the moment and deal with it.

3 Sensitivity is key

Be honest, but don't be tactless. While there's no point in fibbing to spare her feelings when she clearly knows the score, there's no need to go on about how her crush was in hysterics over it, either. Be sensitive to your friend's feelings, stem your own laughter and put yourself in her position.

4 Minimise embarrassment

Your pal's emerged from the toilet with her skirt tucked into the back of her knickers. Don't yell across the room – signal discreetly from the other side or run up, give her a hug and casually untuck it at the same time.

5 Think positive

Don't dwell on what's happened. Find ways of cheering her up, like "remember when…" stories. Remember when your deputy head broke his chair in assembly? Remember when the school hottie's trousers split at the bum and exposed his boxers? Embarrassing things happen to everyone!

6 Act now, laugh later

There's no denying that embarrassing moments are funny and, at some point afterwards, your pal will hopefully be ready to laugh at their own mishaps. However, it's knowing when to giggle that's important. One hour after it's happened? Too soon. One week, and you're probably safe!

Curly girlie

I wanted to look my best for my birthday party, so I went to the hairdresser to get a cool curly 'do. The stylist had just finished putting loads of rollers in, when suddenly the fire alarm went off. I was ushered out into the street looking like a batty old granny with all my rollers in, just as a bunch of fit lads walked by!

Chantal, East Sussex

Peeping Tom!

I'd been shopping for a dress for my mate's party and ended up running late, so I had no time to go home and change. I told Mum I'd get ready in the car on the way there. As I was trying to get my new frock on, she had to stop at some traffic lights. And, as she did, a busful of boys pulled up beside us, including my ex, Tom. One lad saw me and nudged his pal. Soon, the whole bus was laughing at me in the back seat in just my undies and tights!

Emily, Milton Keynes

Sit down-er

I was a party with my friends and my crush was lounging on a chair in the corner. He started checking me out and seemed to be beckoning me over to me to sit on his lap. I walked over and sat down, and said, "How's it going?" in my flirtiest voice. He looked really shocked and I turned around to see another girl – his girlfriend – standing there looking annoyed. Mega-cringe or what?

Kia, Peterborough

An untimely exit

I was at a party and spotted a really cute boy. Even better, he seemed to have noticed me, too, so I gave him a flirty smile and hair-flick, then leaned up against the wall, trying to look cool and casual. Except it wasn't a wall, but a fire exit door. It flew open and I fell out. The door slammed shut, locking me out, so I had to walk all the way around the building to the main entrance – in the pouring rain. I ended up looking like a drowned rat – not that it mattered – the cutie had scarpered after seeing what a klutz I am!

Ruth, Southampton

Musical stares

I was at a party with my gang, and had just met a pal's new boyfriend for the first time. Never one to keep my opinions to myself, I said to my bezzie, "Rob's totally gorgeous – well, I'd snog him anyway!" almost having to shout to be heard over the music. You've guessed it, the record stopped suddenly at that point and my other pal, and Rob, heard everything! Lucky for me, she realised I just meant it as a compliment, so no catfight alert. Phew!

Emma, London

Clowning around

I was at my little sister's fifth birthday party and, as a surprise, my Mum had invited a special guest. No one knew who it was and my sister was really excited. Then, out of nowhere sprang a clown with a big red nose and face-paint. I screamed hysterically and ran out of the room. Later, I had a go at Mum, telling her she knew I have a phobia of clowns. "I thought you'd outgrown it," she said. Obviously not!

Kim, Leeds

. . . .

DJ disaster

My friend had hired a hall and a DJ for her birthday. We were all dancing and having a great time when I decided to ask the DJ to play one of our fave songs and dedicate it to her. On my way up to the stage, I tripped over a wire and fell over. I thought no one had noticed until suddenly the music cut out. When I'd tripped up I'd accidentally pulled out the power cable!

mizz **fan, Berkshire**

Ice scream

My best mate's family had just moved into a new house and, to celebrate, they threw a housewarming party. While all the adults chatted in the kitchen, we girls went into the living room to watch a movie, with loads of popcorn and ice cream. It was fun 'til a scary bit made me jump, and I spilled half-melted chocolate ice cream all over her parents' brand new sofa and carpet!

Daisy, Cambridge

New Year's eek!

My friend invited me to her place on New Year's Eve as her parents were holding a big bash. It was going really well until I went upstairs to use the bathroom, after we'd welcomed the new year in. The door was open so I walked straight in – and, to my horror, saw her elderly granddad sitting stark naked in the bath! It was really not a good start to the new year!

Marie, Bude

Fang-cy dress

I'd fancied a lush lad in my class for ages, and last year he held a massive party over Halloween weekend, and I was invited. I really wanted to make a good impression, so my mate and I decided to go all out on our vampire costumes. We even had fake blood dripping from our fags. To our embarrassment, we arrived to find everyone else in really posh outfits! No one had told us it was a black-tie do and not fancy dress as we'd assumed!

Sarah, Heathfield

Egghead

My little bro was having a party and I'd invited my crush along to help out. We were in the garden organising egg and spoon races, when one of the kids who had lost started getting really upset. He picked up his spoon and catapulted his egg into the air. Before I could shout out, it hit my crush right in the head! Ouch…

Miranda, Devon

Frock horror!

Some friends and I were taking the bus to a party at our village hall, and, distracted by the sight of my crush and his mates waiting outside, I didn't take care as I got off. As I went down the steps from the upper deck, one of my kitten heels caught in the hem of my long dress. As well as falling over, I had to spend the rest of the evening in a dress that was ripped all the way up to my bum!

Katie, Newcastle

Too early, girlie!

I was spending New Year's Eve with my family, and my brother thought it would be really funny to wind my watch forward by an hour. So, at just before 11pm, I got all excited and started counting down, then sang *Auld Lang Syne* at the top of my voice. Everyone thought I was a complete weirdo! Oops!

Gemma, Loughborough

Left out

One night, my parents went out and let my elder sis and me have a few friends over – and we made the most of being home alone, playing our music really loud. Halfway through the night, I nipped outside to call our cat in 'cause it was cold, but when I rang the doorbell to get back in, nobody could hear me over the din. I ended up shivering on the doorstep for almost an hour 'til someone noticed I was missing. Some great friends I've got, eh?

Sevanna, by email

What the devil…?

My friend loves Halloween, so when she decided to throw a party for it, she went all out. We decorated the house with loads of spooky stuff, including a life-sized model of a red devil, which must have had motion sensors – because as I walked past it, it suddenly let out a piercing screech then started cackling. I leapt backwards in shock, and got tangled up in a load of fake cobwebs!

Lara, East Sussex

Lost!

I spent last New Year's Eve at a huge fireworks display at a country club near my home. It was pitch black and I got separated from my parents. I couldn't find them anywhere so I went to find one of the attendants. They put out an announcement across the loud speaker saying "a little girl called Suzie has lost her mummy and daddy"! I was so embarrassed, especially when I saw some boys from my school in the front row!

Suzie, Tetbury

Barf bash

I was at my parents' anniversary party and we'd had a huge meal and loads of dessert. At the end of the night, as people started to leave, everyone was hugging and saying their goodbyes. I started to feel really sick from all I'd eaten and threw up all over my friend's dad. I can still picture the total disgust on everyone's face!

Charlotte, Derby

Netball nightmare

I'd just started at a new school and been picked for the netball team, so I invited everyone I knew to come and support me at my first match. It was about to start when the girl I was marking said, 'Eww, look at that woman's coat – ug-lee!' When I looked up I saw my Mum wearing the most hideous, fluorescent green coat! As if that wasn't bad enough, she was also holding a banner with my name on so everyone knew I was her daughter!

Helena, Southampton

Daddy uncool!

My folks had let me go to a teen disco on condition that
I let Dad come and collect me at 10pm. I was just about
to leave to meet him, when the DJ started playing my fave
song – so I decided Dad could wait for five more minutes
while I danced to it. I was bopping away when someone
tapped me on the shoulder. Thinking it'd be a hot lad
asking me to dance, I put on my best smile and turned
around. To my horror, it was Dad! Instead of waiting outside
with the other parents, he'd come in to find me! Argh!

Charlene, Oxford

Keeping mum

I was shopping with my mum when I bumped into my
crush. We started chatting but then Mum butted in and
asked, "Don't I get an introduction, then?" Embarrassed,
I said, "Mum, meet Luke, Luke, this is my mum," only for
her to start gushing, "Oh, so *you're* Luke! Michelle hasn't
been able to stop talking about you!' I was so humiliated
I just stood there going bright red!

Michelle, Brighton

Lunchbox laughter

Every weekday, my dad drops me off at school. One morning, I'd just got out of the car and crossed the road, when I heard the horn beeping. I turned round to see Dad leaning out of the car window, shouting "Hey, Georgie-Porgie, you forgot your lunchbox!" Everyone around me started laughing, and some of the lads even started singing *Georgie-Porgie Pudding And Pie* at me! It'll be ages before I'm allowed to forget it, too!

Georgina, Chester

Wait for it…

Recently, our school held a themed cheese and wine evening for all the parents, and the pupils had to come in fancy dress and be the waiters and waitresses. We were all standing in our designated areas when someone started giggling. I turned round to see my parents arriving, dressed in really mad '70s gear, including massive party wigs! They'd thought that parents were supposed to come dressed up too! How embarrassing!

Jessica, Broughton

Sore loser

At school, we did a project on the Victorians and I was really proud of mine because I'd worked so hard on it. A few weeks after handing it in, there was an awards ceremony, and all the parents were invited. When another girl got awarded the prize for the best project, my dad yelled really loudly, "That's not fair!" I was so embarrassed I pretended I didn't know him.

Beth, Essex

Bank blush

As I was trying to pay some money in at the bank, the cashier said to me, really quietly, that they couldn't accept the card. I got really angry and said, "Do I look like I would commit fraud?" and she replied, really calmly, "Well you're certainly not a boy." I didn't get what she meant 'til I snatched the card back and realised I'd picked up my brother's by mistake! Everyone in the queue was staring at me like I was crazy, and I don't blame them!

Tammy, Kent

Oh, the iron-y!

One day I was in a rush to go out, so I begged my sis to iron my top while I did my hair and make-up. She looked a bit awkward when she brought it to my room but I just grabbed it, flung it on and dashed off out. When I met my mate half an hour later, she said, 'There's a huge hole burnt in the back off your top!" I was mortified – you could see my bra strap! I didn't speak to my sis for over a week.

Ruby, Cheshire

Dad's got the cringe factor

I was shopping with my family and, as we were going up the escalator in a store, my dad decided to burst into song. Everyone stopped to stare at him singing *Somewhere Over The Rainbow* in a silly, high-pitched voice while I ran into a shop, crying with embarrassment! I sulked all day and refused to speak to my dad for humiliating me like that!

Rosa, by email

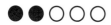

Mama, don't dance!

I was at my school's summer fete with my mum one weekend when I bumped into my mates. I decided to go off with them for a while to see if we could spot my crush. After walking around for a bit, we heard a crowd of people cheering. To my horror, my mum and my crush were dancing together! I haven't let her come anywhere near my school since!

Vanessa, London

Toddler trauma

My mum and I took my toddler brother to the park, but, as he's only little, he'd just run off whenever we weren't looking. One time, he ran right into the middle of the park, pulled down his trousers and stood there in his nappy, giggling. It was so embarrassing as the park was packed and I was the one who had to go and get him!

Kerri, Scotland

....

Naughty nan

We were out with our nan, to watch her friend line-dancing in the town square – then we were told we had to join in! We lined up at the back, hoping not to be noticed, but then Nan's friend called our names out over the microphone, and we were forced to stand right at the front of the group. After the dance ended, we glanced over at Nan. She and her friends – and everyone else – were laughing! A pants end to a rubbish day!

Lindsey and Charlotte, Sheffield

That's hot!

For my birthday, my family went for a curry, and my Dad and brother both ordered the spiciest dish. I ordered something different, but when it arrived, it had hardly any veg in it. My brother heard me moaning and offered me his green beans. I took a big mouthful and wondered why he was laughing. It turned out they were chillies, and so hot I began choking – so everyone else in the restaurant turned round to stare. Brotherly love? Yeah, right!

Amelia, Birmingham

Shelving shambles

I was shopping for jeans with my sister when she saw a pair she really liked. The only thing was, they were on a the highest shelf. There weren't any shop assistants around to help us, so she jumped up and grabbed them herself. Not only did the pair of jeans she was after come down, but so did the entire shelf with all the other pairs, too! All we could manage was a mumbled apology, before we ran out of the shop!

Sarah, East Sussex

Limo dimbo

For my cousin's birthday party, we went to the cinema and, to make it even more of a treat, her parents hired a limo for us to all go in! After the film finished, we went back to her house for more fun and games... But, when we all got out of the limo, my foot caught in a seatbelt and I fell face-first on to the pavement! The shame…

Lottie, by email

A bum deal!

I was out in town with my mum and toddler bro when a boy about my age walked past us. My bro reached out and smacked him on his bum, while shouting "Bum, bum, bum!" I don't know who was cringing more, the lad or Mum and me!

Shelley, by email

• •

Slumber blunder

I went to a sleepover last week and, before we settled down to watch the DVD we'd rented, we all changed into our pyjamas. Mine felt really tight but I managed to squeeze into them, only to see that the legs just came down to my knees and the sleeves to my elbows. My mates started laughing and I soon realised that my Mum had packed my little sister's PJs in my bag by mistake! I had to sleep in my tee and knickers!

Laura, Cornwall

Dealing with embarrassing people

Often, it's our nearest and dearest – close friends and family – who trigger the biggest blushes in day-to-day life. Here's how to cope with them and bin the cringe for good....

Cringey parents

So, you have a dad who comes to pick you up in front of all your mates or a mum who still calls you Babykins?

Bin the cringe Your parents aren't superheroes, they're people, just like you, so don't be hard on them. Whether they make you mad, embarrass you by snorting with laughter or yell at you in front of your new boyfriend... Stop. Take a deep breath and cut them some well-deserved slack – they only act like they do 'cause they care so much about you. And, face it, you could be much worse off. Look at the mums you see in soaps, like Gail and Sally in *Corrie*. Bet yours isn't anything like as bad!

A blush-making bezzie

Your best mate has blabbed to your crush that you doodle his name in your notepad and dream about him every night – how do you recover from humiliation like that?

Bin the cringe Just brush it off! Try laughing at yourself, making a joke about the situation, or ignoring it altogether. Unless it's an extremely visible mistake, most of the time the other person won't even pay attention to it unless you make it a big deal of it. So, you like him and he's found out about it – so what? If he's into you, it may be the push he needs to ask you out, knowing it's unlikely he'll be rejected. So spare your pal the hissy fit!

The smoochy boyfriend

Your boyfriend is always trying to hold your hand and snog you in public and it's starting to embarrass you big time...

Bin the cringe Some girls would love to be in this situation, but if you're not fond of PDAs – public displays of affection – tell him tactfully. Say you like your lovey-dovey moments to be special and private between the two of you, and not paraded in front of bus queues, your neighbours or – please, no! – your folks! Be honest about how you feel and hopefully he'll understand.

The overprotective older brother

A boy just needs to look at you and big bro starts growling...

Bin the cringe OK, so you're his baby sis, and it's only natural for him to feel concern for your safety and well-being, but, while he may think he's looking out for you, he's actually destroying any ounce of street cred you ever had. Having him jump in between you at the first inkling of a snog is *so* not cool – in fact, it's downright cringey!

Older siblings need to realise that they can't protect you forever. You need to make your own decisions, and even your own mistakes, or how else will you learn about life! Talk to your bro – he may not realise how OTT he can be at times. Tell him you don't want him to end up like Warren or Calvin from *'Oaks*!

Toilet trouble

My class went on a residential trip and lots of girls-vs-boys wind-ups went on. One night, my mate ran into their dorm and took a pic of them in their PJs and undies. They wanted revenge and busted into our dorm, flinging the bathroom door open – while I was on the loo! One lad snapped a pic of me sat on it – luckily, he deleted it after I begged him to, but I still cringe thinking about it!

Hannah, Surrey

Girlie gossip

One weekend I was having a major girlie crisis, so I decided to ring my bezzie for advice. I was so relieved when she picked up, that I just blurted out loads of stuff about my periods. When I finally finished, I heard a boy laughing at the other end of the phone. My mate had left her mobile in the kitchen and her brother had answered it! I haven't been able to face him since!

Danielle, Banbury

Jump around!

My class were having a gym lesson at school, using the trampoline. It was great fun then, all of a sudden, I felt a ping as my bra came undone! It started flapping around under my T-shirt and my hopes that nobody would notice were a bit unrealistic. All the laughs as I ran off to the changing room to do it up again told me that!

Amanda, Kent

●●○○○

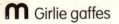

Under-where?

We'd just finished our swimming class and I was drying off when I realised I'd lost my knickers. I was panicking that I wasn't going to find them, when my teacher held them up in the middle of the changing rooms and shouted, "Has anyone lost a pair of white knickers? I was so embarrassed that I didn't say anything and had to go knickerless for the rest of the day!

Jodie, Sheffield

Dad madness

For my 12th birthday, I had a massive party in our village hall. It was all going great until the DJ stopped and my Dad got up on stage. Everything went quiet and he started making this huge speech about how he couldn't believe how grown-up I'd become, and how it seemed like only yesterday that I was wetting the bed! I could feel myself going redder and redder as he went on to tell a load of embarrassing stories about me. Needless to say, my mates found it hilarious! Thanks, Dad!

Poppy, Hertfordshire

Dating d'oh!

I was at the cinema with my new boyfriend and, 'cause he'd got the tickets, I insisted on paying for the popcorn. "My treat," I said, opening my purse, only for him to see the photo-pocket inside it – which still contained a pic of my rather weird celeb crush, Bradley from *'Enders*, dotted with sparkly heart stickers. He kept sniggering all through the film and it wasn't even a comedy!

Amanda, Coventry

Just desserts

My crush had finally asked me out and, for our date we went to an all-you-can-eat buffet. He was saying how he couldn't stand girls who just ordered salads and picked at their food, so I helped myself to a really big portion and really tucked in. The meal was going great 'til I began to get really bad indigestion. I was in so much pain I had to ask him to take me home early!

Kimberley, East Peckham

Gone with the wind

As I was walking to school one day, my bags felt really heavy, so I decided to have a little rest and bent over to put them on the ground for a minute. Unfortunately, the wind caught my skirt and blew it right up, revealing my pants! And, of course, this was the busiest time of day, so loads of people, including a bus queue full of boys from my school, had a right old laugh at me!

Brittany, Surrey

Handbag horror

When I was on holiday, I went shopping with my mum and stepdad in the local town. There were loads of little stores there and for some reason, all the shopkeepers were giving me strange looks. It wasn't 'til I looked down that I realised I'd been fiddling with the charm on my bag and had accidentally pulled open the front pocket, which was full of tampons!

Melissa, by email

Brace yourself

I was standing at my coach stop and there were some older girls who kept whispering to each other and looking at me. I could feel my brace plate coming out of my mouth, so I turned around and pushed it back in. Unfortunately, when I took my hand away, my brace got caught on my woolly glove, and then got accidentally flung over to where the girls were standing!

Lauren, by email

 Girlie gaffes

Peek-ini

I was in the garden, enjoying the sunshine and lovin' the new bikini I was wearing – as well as looking fab it had been a real bargain. So, when my brother's gorgeous mates came over to see him, I strutted into the kitchen to say hi to them. But, as I walked in, one of the straps snapped and I ended up flashing them instead! I found out the tough way that it had been cheap for a reason!

Liz, Tunbridge Wells

Footsie oopsy

When we got our new seating plan at school, I was thrilled to hear I'd been allocated a desk next to the lad I fancy. As we sat down for class, I felt something brush against my foot. Assuming it was his foot, I kept touching it with mine – and felt so chuffed that he made no attempt to move it. Too bad I realised after a while that it was just his school bag! I still feel too embarrassed to fess about it to my mates, so I thought I'd tell *mizz* instead!

Heather, Bristol

Gum chums

I was on a date with this really cute boy and he'd gone to the loo. I knew he'd want to kiss me at some point, so I popped some minty chewing gum into my mouth to freshen my breath. He was just about to lean in for the all-important moment, when I realised I'd forgotten to spit my gum out. By that time, I had no choice but to kiss him, and, by the end of the snog my gum had somehow made its way into his mouth – gross!

Katie, Hull.

Snot a good look

Last weekend, I bumped into my crush in town. I was really pleased as it meant I finally had a chance to speak to him alone. I started asking him how his week had been and what he was up to, but he seemed to be in a hurry and kept making excuses to leave. It was only when I was walking out of the shop and I caught my reflection in the mirror, that I realised I had a massive bogey hanging from my nose! Very attractive – not!

Amy, Shropshire

Fame shame

I was in London for the day, when I saw a really glamorous woman with long blonde hair and massive sunnies. I was convinced she was famous and, as I got closer I suddenly realised who she was. Excited, I ran up and said, "Hi, Paris! It's so great to meet you, can I have your autograph?" She gave me a really strange look, said, 'Sorry, I'm not Paris Hilton!' then walked off. Blush alert!

Sophie, by email

Underwater undies

I went swimming with my club from school and we'd just jumped into the pool, when someone asked if I had forgotten to take my knickers off. I looked down to see my bright pink knickers practically glowing through my white swimsuit. Yikes!

Lucy, Oxford

Windy-pops!

We were at a party when my friend suggested playing some games. The first involved two teams racing to pass a balloon over their heads and through their legs. I was really excited because I was in the same team as the boy I fancied. When the balloon reached me, I grabbed it and bent over to pass it back to him, but just as he did, I let out a big fart, right in his face! He was so shocked, he jumped backwards, popping the balloon and making a huge scene in front of everyone! Bad night…

Emma, York

Shower error

Our school went on a trip and one day, feeling a bit sweaty, I took a shower. I came out with a towel wrapped around me, no make-up on and mascara smudged under my eyes. As I looked up, I saw a whole group of boys in our room, sat talking with my mates! My friend had invited them over without warning me! Everyone laughed so I dashed back into the bathroom. Whoops!

Hayley Oxford

Time to lie low...

When I was on holiday with my family on the Greek island of Kos, my sister and I bought a big pink lilo and headed straight for the beach. While I was swimming underwater, I spotted the lilo above me, so I swam up and pushed it over. When I stood up, I saw my sister laughing at me from the sand, and a very wet, angry lady – with an identical lilo – standing in front of me!

Beth, Balsall Common

Carousel capers

We were at the airport waiting for our luggage when I spotted my case on the carousel, so I went over and grabbed it, pulling it as hard as I could. It was heavier than I remembered and, as soon as it was clear of the conveyor belt, I dropped it. Suddenly, I heard this massive yelp, and I looked up to see a man with his eyes watering. My case had landed right on his foot!

Alison, Edinburgh

●●●○○

Food flight

I was on a plane to America and had ended up sitting next to a really cute boy. I was psyching myself up to chat to him when the cabin crew came to give us our food. As I was in a window seat, I reached over the lad to take the tray. Suddenly, there was loads of turbulence, I lost my grip and food flew everywhere, covering him in it! The only time I ended up speaking to him was to apologise throughout the rest of the flight!

Justine, Newcastle

Biking blunder

During my family's camping holiday, we all decided to go for a bike ride. While we were cycling along, I spotted a really cute boy ahead of us. I was so preoccupied with staring at him that I didn't concentrate on what I was doing and lost control of my bike! The next thing I knew, I was sitting on my bum in a ditch!

Victoria, Sidcup

Sea-through

My friend and I were chilling out on the beach when we decided it'd be funny to go in the sea with all our clothes on. The problem was, we totally forgot were both wearing white tops, so as soon as we went in they went totally see-through. And, as it was the middle of a hot, sunny day, we had to walk past loads of people when we eventually plucked up the courage to leave the water!

Katrina, Pembrokeshire

Game over!

On holiday in Turkey, my friend and I noticed a big game of beach volleyball about to start, so we went to see if we could join in. There were some really hot lads playing so we wanted them to take notice of us. About halfway through the game, someone gave a really good serve and I had to dive to get it. I ended up missing the ball and crashing straight into the pole bringing down the whole net with me and getting a nosebleed! Ouch…

Lucy, Manchester

Hanging around

Our class went for a day out at an adventure centre, something I was totally excited about. When we got there, we were set a challenge to launch ourselves off the top of a high slope, grab a bar and then swing down. When it was my go, I jumped but forgot to grab the bar. I just dangled in mid-air from my safety harness for ages 'til an instructor helped me down. Major blushes!

Hannah, Rotherham

In-flight entertainment

My family were on the flight back from our holiday and my Mum bought my sister and me headphones for the plane. I was listening to my favourite song when my Mum tapped me on the shoulder. I'd been singing along loudly without even realising it. When I took my headphones off, people in the row in front of me were actually applauding!

Abbie, Aylesbury

Jersey jumble

I was camping in Cornwall when I saw a really fit boy who was wearing the same top as one my brother had. When I came back to the campsite, I found my bro and started telling him all about this gorgeous lad I'd seen wearing "his" jumper. Suddenly he turned around and I realised it wasn't my brother at all – I was face to face with the fittie! He was staying on the same campsite as us!

Elsa, Basingstoke

Photo flopper

I recently went on a sailing holiday with my family around the Caribbean. We stopped in a really nice location and everyone was jumping off the boat, so I decided I'd do a really good dive off the side. Preparing to take the plunge, I asked my mum to take a photo of me in action, but, at the last minute, I hesitated and ended up doing a belly flop! When I broke the surface, all I heard was "Ooh, painful!" – and they weren't wrong!

Sophie, Exeter

Back out!

On a holiday in America, my family visited a water park. My mum and I were standing next to each other while the powerful wave machine began. A wave hit me and, underwater, I grabbed for my mum's leg and held on to it as I tried to stand up again. When I finally caught my breath, I saw my family, including my mum, laughing at me as I clung on to what was actually the lifeguard's leg!

Dion, Cumbria

Bruised ego

As we walked back to our hotel at the end of a day's sightseeing, the flags flying on the top of the building caught my eye. As I tried to remember which countries they represented – all the while trying to keep up with my parents – I didn't focus on where I was going, and walked right into a lamp-post. Embarrassing enough, but I also had to spend the rest of the holiday walking around with two black eyes!

Rachel, Sudbury

Toilet trauma

I was camping in France with my dad and needed to use the portable toilets on the site. Seeing one was vacant, I pushed the door – only to see an old man sat on the loo because the lock on the door had broken! He looked all shocked and confused and started to shout at me in French. I went back to my tent and waited for another half-hour so I could be sure he was gone. I've never felt so awkward in my life!

Alisha, Stoke-on-Trent

It's snow joke!

During the last school hols, I went skiing with my family. When I got on to the slopes, I started going down a really easy ski run but, when my sister called to me, I lost my concentration and my skis crossed! I overbalanced, fell flat on my face and went skidding. My skis flew off in different directions and I slid down the rest of the slope on my front! My sister was wetting herself laughing!

Mary, Westmeath.

Surf's up

On holiday in Cornwall, I tried to impress some local hotties by telling them I could surf. Things went great 'til they invited me to come surfing with them, and I nervously agreed – I mean, how difficult could it be? I soon found out when I went crashing off the board and came up gasping for air, with the boys' laughter ringing in my ears. I'll never lie to big myself up again!

Liz, Taunton

Dizzy heights

My family went on holiday and we hiked up a massive, craggy hill. I'm really scared of heights and, as we were walking, I started to feel a bit wobbly. I made it to the top but when they made me look over the edge, I threw up! So gross!

Lilly, Devon